jessica tames

other books by jessica tames

never get mad at a fish
twenty something
selfish
don't pretend it didn't happen
in case of emergency, crack spine
'til the end
golden
open heart surgery

for myself
because i deserve to be happy
and for you
because you do too

"and if i'm flying solo, at least i'm flying free…"

—elphaba, *wicked the musical*

if she'd ended it all at just eighteen
she would not be here today
to tell her story
what a tragedy
that would be

i was twelve the first time i looked at a girl differently
she was tall
big boned
with long dark hair
mischievous brown eyes
and a smile that could put even the most innocent of angels to shame

i remember wanting to be by her side at every waking moment
and whenever i wasn't
i would find myself wondering what she was up to
who she was with
and whether she was thinking about me too

my therapist asks me
"do you have a crush on her?"
and all i can think is
"if 'crush' means i want to spend the rest of my life with her, then yes"

suddenly the realization hits me like a wave of truth
into a new soul i no longer recognize
i like girls
i like girls a lot
but i shouldn't
i can't
what will they think?
will i still be safe at school?
at home?

am i still the same me?

i'm sorry
i whisper as i regress deeper and deeper
but this is what i want to do
want to?
it whispers back knowingly
or have to?

the bathroom stall is cramped and humid
but i stay there
knowing that if i come out
(no pun intended)
i would have to face what i'd been trying so hard to shove back down

i think i'm bisexual, i type
she types back, **how do u know?**
there are beautiful girls everywhere i turn
i've never looked at them in this way before
everyone feels that way at some point
it's normal
then why am i getting so emotional over it?

i never got an answer

denial ≠ fiction
denial = avoiding the facts

sexuality isn't hard to understand
but the way some people talk about it
it might as well be calculus

you said to me
that i shouldn't go around
and tell people i'm gay
but i'd only be doing it
to protect myself

you don't "agree" with it
but you haven't disowned me
so that counts
for something

never in a million years
did i think that
peer pressure
could apply to
one's sexuality

to you
it's sad that
i didn't turn out
the way you wanted me to

to me
it's sad that
you had too unrealistic expectations

after all
i was always
a master
at playing pretend

early on in our relationship
i learned not to trust you
still i stayed
because somehow
distrust was better
than being alone

it was may 24, 2018
we'd just gotten back from dinner
i knew it was now or never

what i didn't know was
where i'd end up
if your reaction was
anything but positive

but alas
i tearfully called you into my room
and said i had to tell you something

when the words left my lips
tears fell from my eyes
a frightened child
desperately seeking her mother's approval

or at the very least
whatever love she had to give me

i should've ended things
as soon as the thought came to my mind
but i couldn't bear to hurt you
not yet

when i finally told you what i'd been hiding
you tearfully asked me if you were holding me back
and maybe i shouldn't have lied
but maybe you shouldn't have believed me

all i ever wanted
was for you to understand
that sometimes
no matter how hard we try
we are physically incapable
of pleasing one another

you don't accept me
you can't
you won't
and i have to accept that

if being gay was a choice
whyever on god's green earth
would anyone

choose

to be hated
simply for who we love?

it's a funny thing
how when one door is bolted shut
another one comes swishing open
with the force of a thousand winds

never did i expect you
to appear when i needed you most
but then again
i suppose that's why i call you my angel

stay with me
and i promise
i will make your new home
worth your while

i didn't merely ask for you
i wished for you
begged for you
pleaded
and the universe
eventually
gave me everything i ever wanted
and more

it's not that i'm
in love with you
or anything
it's just that

if given the chance

i would lasso the moon
and hand it to you
on a silver platter

silly me
for thinking that
you'd ever accept me
for anything less than
who you always
wanted me
to be

i'd always wanted to be
a good mother
until the day i realized
i might not ever get the chance
to even be
a mother

i don't know
what you want from me
because all i hear
is you telling me
how worthless i am

if you ever
decide to
accept this part of me
i want you to know
that it will
no longer
matter
because
i've already
accepted
myself
and that
is what
matters

not even my
daily dose of caffeine
can wash out the
sour taste
your kiss left
in my mouth

and darling
before you start
doubting your worth
remind yourself
that you are here
now
and you did not
get here
by way of
weakness

they lack the kindness
you wish to spread
and it isn't your fault
they refuse to change

nothing lasts forever
and you
will be
okay
someday

even the
smallest of deeds
are noticed by
the ones who really
care

being you
is so much more
rewarding
than trying so hard
to be
anyone else

don't settle
for less than
you deserve
especially
when you are told
you don't deserve
anything

keep trying
even if it's just
to spite the ones
who told you
you can't

some people will be
unable to see
your worth
that doesn't mean
it isn't there

reach your goals
for yourself
and let their wrongful doubt
fizzle out slowly
(but make sure they're watching)

don't let them
take over your mind
so much so
that you lose
the progress that
you already made

if
"scars are stories"
then why
do i seem
to have
writer's block?

it's gotten to the point
where i can't imagine
a life without you
and oh god
i hope you stay

in the quiet of my room
i slip my hands beneath the covers
with her
and only her
on my mind

i guess
the one good thing
about all this
is that
i have finally
accepted myself
and others' opinions
mean nothing to me
anymore

you speak
so negatively
of yourself
and i wish
so badly
that i could
take your insecurities
and squash them like a bug
in the palm of my hand
while i hold you
with the other

no
i have not always
been this confident
yes
the long journey
was worth it

it's true what they say
how spilling your burdens
out onto paper
makes them easier
to bear

never will i understand
the bitter souls who spew hate
onto the ones who love loudly

if only
there was some
magic potion to
make the pain go away
at least for a little while

oh that's right
i'm afraid to touch it
for fear that i will
become just like you

don't stop giving
no matter how much
the world takes
from you

slowly but surely
she grew into the woman
she was destined to be

why is it
that the ones who are
supposed to
shower you
with love
are the same ones who
can snatch their love
away from you
just as quickly?

i'm so glad
we can be
so forward
with each other
and it's not
uncomfortable
in the slightest

i would rather
have each one of my eyelashes
ripped out by the root
than lose you

she makes me melt
so often
you'd think i was
built from butter

i will
no longer accept
anything less than
what makes me
happy

my soul is
yours now
be gentle with it

you occupy
every corner of my mind
with the way you
simply
are

yes
i do know
what i did to you
i do know
how wrong it was
i don't know
how else to say i'm sorry

i'm almost home
my love
i'll be there
soon

i find comfort
in the silence now
because i know
you will remain
waiting
on the other end

i want to know
your whole story
so i will wait
forever
for you to
tell it to me

it happened so fast
but i think
it was what
we needed

there are some things
i won't forget about you
that i'd rather not remember

and there are somethings
i won't remember about you
that i'd rather not forget

you were not a mistake
you were a lesson
that i learned
just in time

upon hearing those
awful
vile
inexcusable
words leave your mouth
i vow to myself
that i will
never be
like you

i sit here
wondering when
you will tell them
about us

i sit here
knowing that
i'm guilty of
the exact same thing

we got to
know each other
in reverse

first we asked the
deep cuts
then we rewound to
the icebreakers

and quite frankly
i liked
that way
a lot better

if ever
there comes a time
where we need to
run away
together
just know
i'll be
ready
whenever
you are

i think
my heart
always knew
it needed you

it just took
my brain
a little longer
to figure it out

i feel
free
so very
free

acknowledgements

mom: your endless support means the world to me.

lexie: you're my everything, angel.

my fellow instapoets: thank you for encouraging me every step of the way.

Made in United States
North Haven, CT
30 December 2021